Build My List,

Build My Business,

Build My Bank Account!

CATAPULT My Business To Super Success Series Blueprint!

Using List Building Strategies, Email Marketing, Webinars and much more to Track and Watch Your INCOME GROW!

Shelley Mitchell, *BA, ACC, CPM, CAPS, CAM, MORS, COS, HCCP*

Shelley Mitchell, BA, ACC, CPM, CAPS, CAM, HCCP, COS, MORS

DEDICATION

This workbook is dedicated to my amazing clients who push me every single day to continue to grow so I can continue to create the resources to provide to them so I can then proceed to "kick their butt" (as they lovingly state is WHY they work with me) and build their businesses – THEIR DREAM -... And just as important, I dedicate this to my family who continues to put up with me and still LOVE ME even when I'm totally HYPERFOCUSED on helping my clients, creating new things and building my business - MY DREAM – all the while there are no groceries or clean clothes in the house and they've stopped allowing me in the kitchen because it rarely ends well.

Build My List, Build My Business, Build My Bank Account!
Catapult Your Business to Super Success Series Blueprint
Using List Building Strategies, Email Marketing, Webinars and much more to
Track and Watch Your Income Grow!

CONTENTS

	Acknowledgments	7
1	My Personal Business List Building Tracker	13
2	My Personal Business List Building Basics	15
3	My Personal Business List Building Strategy	21
4	My Personal Business Marketing PLANNING Strategy	23
5	Email Planning Sheet Template	25
6	Guest Invitation Template	27
7	Follow up with potential guests who haven't replied Template	29
8	WEBINAR email announcement template	31
9	Webinar reminder email Template	33
10	SOCIAL MEDIA AND PRESS RELEASE POSTS - TEMPLATES	35
11	Webinar Checklist / Agenda	39
12	Webinar Thank You email TEMPLATE	41
	Joint Teleseminar PLANNER	42
	About the Author - Shelley	45
	Get Your Free Weekly Success Planner Here	47

MyPersonalBusinessCoach.com

Shelley Mitchell, BA, ACC, CPM, CAPS, CAM, HCCP, COS, MORS

ACKNOWLEDGMENTS

With great appreciation to Melissa Ingold with Time Freedom Business for sharing her scripts but with tremendous acknowledgement and appreciation to one of my mentors and Business Coach, Michele Scism. She has provided things to me put in a simple way I could understand, just when I thought all was lost and I was totally confused. I started following her before I even started my own business and love that she helps so many people grow six figure businesses by sharing her knowledge whole heartedly, knowing her own true value partnered with a lot of TOUGH LOVE.

Build My List – Build My Business – Build My Bank Account

So many people start their business with wide eyes and high hopes. They're excited to get their business cards, create a logo, buy new colorful folders for their office, put their website in place, and so on.

Entrepreneurs will even invest a lot of money for the basic systems to create logos, branding, etc. In reflecting on what I have learned while going through my career and having my own business, I look back to see some of the things or areas where I really missed the point. I am writing this book to show you what "I wish I knew then what I know now" and to share what one of the big ones is.

We all have strengths and gifts God has given us that we are so innately great at that sometimes we take them for granted. But when we finally get the entrepreneurial bug and we decide to go out and share them with the world, we think that if simply build it, they will come. That's what happens, right? No!!!

What usually happens when we start our own business is that we build it and then no one shows up, except some crickets who stumbled upon us by accident. As coaches spending thousands of dollars going through coaching school, there can be a huge misconception about customers coming just because we are ready for them. Certified coaches spend hundreds or thousands of hours learning how to be great coaches, and then we can't wait to go out and find our first clients. But then after we get out of school and start our own business, we quickly find out that people aren't banging down our doors to work with us. There are times where we can't even give coaching away.

So what do we do? We spend a lot of time and money creating the perfect business card, the perfect welcome packet, the perfect price list, the perfect website and then hours of our time on social media going straight down that rabbit hole never to see the light of day again.

The top two things that no one ever tells us to do are to build our list and to do strategy sessions where we ask for the sale. The second one is told to us, but we are never told ask for the sale. As coaches, we can be afraid to close the sale because we don't want to be rejected and think that as soon as one person says NO, our business will fall to the dust and our dream will completely disintegrate. But let's say you have marketing or sales experience and you were the type of person who had no problem asking for the sale, where do these potential clients come from?

Our list of family and friends is only so long, and social media isn't the best place to establish the value of what it is that you really do. The number one thing I learned that I did not focus

on from the beginning of my business and I wish I knew then is to BUILD MY LIST. Yes, build, track and nurture my list...

Sounds simple? Well it is, but it isn't! You have to build your list, but you have to track it and you have to nurture it; but more importantly, there are several different ways you need to build your list, and I'm going to share some of them with you.

First, you begin to build your list from the original set of contacts you already have. That's your family, friends, colleagues, and people who you already know.

Second, your list is built by the people you know and are going to meet as you are out networking, speaking, and raising awareness for your business. You will learn what you can do for others (and vice-versa) by building relationships while learning about what they do and how they serve others.

Third, and even more importantly, is building your list online, which will be addressed primarily in this book. Gaining contacts into your mailing list from people whom you don't even know can be a tremendous resource and is sometimes the easiest step to accomplish.

I once heard Jack Canfield say that your list is worth one dollar per person of annual revenue to your business. I also heard that he had a list of over million people. What does that tell you? When you have a list of only 2000 people, this means your revenue from that list is only about $2,000 annually. If I want to make $100,000 a year, I'd better figure out a different way to bring in that other $98,000, or I'm going to be up that famous creek without a paddle.

So how do you grow your list? This book will give you some great and SIMPLE ideas, a nice tracker to be able to monitor your list on a weekly basis, some email templates on what to say to nurture people and invite them to a webinar through email and social media, and a great checklist on how to do a teleseminar that I learned from one of my mentors.

What you focus on is what you will grow. I was told this before, and I see how clear that is to me today. If you focus on losing weight, you will lose weight. If you focus on saving money, you will save money. If you focus on having a good relationship with your spouse, you will have a good relationship with your spouse. If you focus on building your list, you WILL build your list.

Included are quite a few ideas on how you can build your list. I have noted the NECESSARY and RECOMMENDED things you should be doing in your small businesses, plus some additional ideas that you may want to try. I recommend that you only pick only a few in the beginning and try them out. Be CONSISTENT, though. Consistency is the key--you cannot just put things up online, but must actually promote them. These items are what are going help you build your list.

Shelley Mitchell, BA, ACC, CPM, CAPS, CAM, HCCP, COS, MORS

If you find yourself with questions or are stuck, please go to the back the book to find my contact information, and you can request a quick consultation. My goal is to ensure that all compelling small business owners who have tremendous strengths and talents will go from being amazing people to amazing business people and really get this "business thing" down. If I can help just one person become successful and do this, then I know that I accomplished the task that God put me on this earth to do. And if I can share my experience while you learn from my mistakes and help one more person, then I have reached my goal. I hope you enjoy this workbook, and hope that you are able to go forth and grow your list in monumental strides.

ONE LAST THOUGHT

List building is not an option; it's not something that you do when you get around to it, have more time, have more money, have more resources/knowledge or when you become more successful. It doesn't matter if you are a Coach, a Lawyer, a Real Estate Agent, a Seamstress, an Energy Healer, a Landscaper, a Baker, a Jeweler, a Doctor, a Financial Advisor, a Travel Agent or someone who is involved in an MLM. It doesn't matter who you are; if you have a business or deal with people, you need to build your list, period! Building your list is something that should be at the top of  your priority list from the very beginning from when you even begin to think about starting a business, or simply working for someone else, but are in sales. List building is the number one thing that you can do to grow your business, grow awareness to position yourself as an expert, grow your bank account and make all the money and have the business of your dreams.

Shelley Mitchell, BA, ACC, CPM, CAPS, CAM, HCCP, COS, MORS

1 - My Personal Business List Building Tracker

GOALS (TRACK AND GROW)
- Minimum 5% increase each month in your list growth
- STRETCH GOAL (I want to MAKE MONEY) – 10% increase each month in list growth

List/Revenue Growth	# Last Report/ month	# Now/this month	Growth Since Last Report	Goal for _____ (month)	Notes
Email List					
Facebook Friends					
Facebook Fans					
Twitter Followers					
LinkedIn Contacts					
Strategy Sessions (MTD)					
Private Clients (Active only MTD)					
Group Clients (MTD)					
Date I Last Emailed My Entire List					
Monthly Revenue	$	$	$	$	

MyPersonalBusinessCoach.com

2 - My Personal Business List Building Basics

Question: Why is email marketing necessary? It's really a lot of work and it's really hard for me to be consistent. Is there anything else I can do?

Shelley's Answer: Well, if you want to be successful, you're going to have to implement some consistency into your business. You don't have to do these things if you don't want to but if you're not going to do them, you need to be willing to find someone who will do them for you. This is very important.

Everyone has an email address these days. Whether they have a computer or not, they have an email address.   The advantage of having an email list and nurturing it are below.
*   Email is personal,
*   Email is powerful,
*   Email is purposeful,
*   Email is targeted,
*   Email is one-on-one, if you do it correctly.
*   #1, all of the above can be AUTOMATED to save YOU TIME AND MONEY!

In order to start your email list, you must subscribe to an email marketing service provider or CRM, which I call a Customer Relationship Manager.

These include:
*   MailChimp,
*   AWeber,
*   Constant Contact, and
*   the one that I use currently is Infusionsoft (which is advanced, pricey and in a different league altogether)

There are many others but the first three are the top three and are pretty much the same as far as services and the cost which is basic. They are great for beginners and most small businesses. **Don't spend a lot of thought into which one is better, ask a lot of people and get stuck in perfectionism.** They truly are extremely similar, and you're not going to go wrong by picking one over the other. I tell my clients to sign up for MailChimp because I can help support them with it because I've already learned how to use it. Either way you're going to have to learn something new if you've never used any one of them.

MyPersonalBusinessCoach.com

BLOGGING

Even if you don't have a website, you should at least have a blog. On your blog, you should have an opt-in box on your blog LINKED to your CRM. Please do not link this to your email. You will drive yourself crazy, and it completely defeats the purpose of the opt-in box or the CRM.

If you like to have a website but feel that the cost is prohibitive or you are technically challenged then you should still get a very inexpensive website and have a teenager put it up for you, so you have a place to put your opt in box. Even if it's just one page says who you are, what you stand for and what you are offering what you're giving away in exchange for someone to give you their name phone number and email address, you are doing great!

START BUILDING YOUR LIST

Below are some ideas for you to start collecting information to build your list in the form of business cards or names, emails and phone numbers. (NOTE: I always make a phone number part of what I receive as that is very valuable to me. Have a phone number can often times DOUBLE the value of that lead)

NECESSITIES are RED and RECOMMENDED are **bolded**:
* For Starters :
* **Start speaking for free.** (always have a call to action, collect names)
* Create a blog.
* Create a podcast.
* **Give a workshop or in-house seminar for a local company, church, or nonprofit.**
* Start teaching your material at your house, adult night school or some place in the community.
* Start coaching or consulting with people for free.
* Start writing articles for blogs or publications.
* Create a website for yourself or your new company.
* Write a column for a niche publication or newspaper.
* **Start an email newsletter.**
* Create a web-based radio show.
* **Do webinars or teleseminars.**
* Start getting publicity.
* Sign up to receive info on free publicity opportunities at www.reporterconnection.com.
* (if you plan to write a book)

Note: Start telling people that you are the author of the upcoming book XYZ. You'll start to get benefits from that and it'll help motivate you to actually write your book.

Shelley Mitchell, BA, ACC, CPM, CAPS, CAM, HCCP, COS, MORS

- **Create Your Website and Start Collecting Names**
  Ways to Optimize Your Website to Capture Names - try some of the following ideas for building your website and your mailing list:
- Choose a URL, ideally one that uses your name or book title (if you are writing a book).
- Look at the websites of bestselling authors or specialists in your genre or field. What are they doing on their websites that works and doesn't work?

Create a list of features that you can adapt for your website.

- Decide which website platform you will use. WordPress is a popular platform that is easy to update and modify. (a BASIC site is all you need unless you have a LOT of products to sell)
- **Create your own website** or hire someone to build a website for you. (go daddy is a perfectly fine beginner site to get you started)
- **Have an email opt-in on every page of your website.**
- State your expertise on your website to maximize SEO.
- (if you are writing a book) Put the book cover on the website.
- (if you are writing a book) Offer a two-for-one deal or a reduced price on other books.
- **Create quizzes.**
- **Run contests or giveaways.**
- **Get testimonials.**
- Install social media widgets on every page.
- Have special landing pages for each social media platform.
- Install analytics tools on every page.

Email: Build Your Database

- **Collect business cards at all of your speeches and other events. The old fishbowl method still works. Hold a drawing for a free book or a free hour of coaching.**
- **Entice people to give you their email addresses by offering content that has value. (Jack Canfield calls this an "ethical bribe.")**
- **Create an e-zine or newsletter that you send out to your list regularly.**
- Create emails about hot topics.
- Share daily or weekly tips.
- **Offer a free e-book, report, story or white paper. (OPT IN)**
- Use email templates that are offered by email companies.
- **Test your email copy to see which topics generate the best response.**

Create and Build Your Social Media Platform

- Begin writing a blog, and then use social media to drive people to your blog. **(USE THIS TO PROMOTE YOUR OPT IN and FREE GIFT)**
- Create a blog using Wordpress.org.
- Buy a copy of Blogging for Dummies.
- **Put "how to" in the titles of your blog posts as often as possible.**
- Use photos and video to attract more attention.
- **Multi-task your material by turning book excerpts into blog posts.**
- **Repurpose content by turning a newsletter or media pitch into a blog post.**
- Use Google Analytics' keywords to identify topic ideas for blog posts.
- Research the blogs of bestselling authors and experts in your genre or field. **What kinds of topics do they address? How often are their blogs updated? What works and doesn't? Create a list of features that you can adapt on your blog.**
- Research influential bloggers in your field and pursue guest blogging opportunities.

Create a Facebook fan/business page

- Ensure your Facebook, Twitter, Google+ and LinkedIn pages have consistent looks and consistent messages.
- **Ensure your website and contact information is available on ALL of your social media sites.**
- **List your Facebook business page as your employer on your personal page which will create an automatic "link" for your friends to click on.**

- Look at the Facebook pages of other experts similar to you. How do they create activity on their pages? What do you like and not like? Create a list of ideas that you can incorporate into your page.
- Find the Facebook pages of the people who have influence with your target audience. Cultivate relationships with them by commenting and liking their posts, when appropriate.
- On your blog, create posts that inspire comments, likes and general activity. Add photos and video.
- **Plan and write posts in advance and set a TIMER for your social media activity each day.**
- Consider Facebook contests.
- Consider Facebook advertising.
- BE ENGAGED! LIKE, COMMENT and SHARE on the pages of the people you want to show support. Your messaging shouldn't always be about YOU but about how you add value to the lives of others. (again SET A TIMER...so you don't get sucked down the rabbit hole)

Shelley Mitchell, BA, ACC, CPM, CAPS, CAM, HCCP, COS, MORS

Create a Twitter account
- Cultivate relationships with influential people.
- Create tweets that inspire comments, retweets and general activity.
- Plan and write your tweets in advance.
- On a weekly basis, tweet your free gift to build your list.

3 - My Personal Business List Building Strategy

1. Understand the power of an image (and video)

- Pixlr.com
- Picmonkey.com
- SnagIt
- Free photos – sxc.hu or morguefile.com

2. OPT IN BOX - Free Report or free gift – (I use the "Weekly Success Planner")

- Share image and link back to website
- Ensure that the NAME, EMAIL and PHONE are required fields
- List your Free Report/Gift in your EMAIL SIGNATURE block of your email and at the end of all correspondence
- Advanced move – have the opt in page on a separate page on your site. Then when you send them there that is all they see.
- Advanced move – create an opt in for a free report that you don't promote on a regular basis – instead you give it to others to use as a bonus for their products/services

3. Teleseminars

- You hosting yourself or guest speaker.
- Have a great image for the opt in page and share that linking back to opt in page.
- Always record the call so you can create a product. This can be done easily on freeconferencing.com or freeconferencecall.com. For webinars and slideshows, I use instantteleseminar.com

4. Assessments/Quizzes (I use "Are you FOCUSED on your Business or Do You Have Business ADHD?)

- Create opt in
- Questions should be asked in a way that points to needing your help/guidance
- Always have a call to action at the end whether it's to do some sort of homework (and you follow up) or to contact you for a free discover call or session to discuss the results

5. Blogging

- Share through social media and your newsletter
- When people come to read your blog they can see your free report

6. Social Media Plan

- Building your audience on social media will naturally build your list because people are curious and they will want to know more. They will go to your site where they see your free report.
- Have a Plan
- Use tools to help you such as hoot suite to post with less time and less effort, or use a VA.

7. Create a challenge

- Ultimate _____ Challenge
- 5 Day _____ Challenge

Shelley Mitchell, BA, ACC, CPM, CAPS, CAM, HCCP, COS, MORS

4 - My Personal Business Marketing PLANNING Strategy

HAVE A PLAN
Annually, Quarterly, Monthly, Weekly & Daily

1. BLOCK OFF big events for the year IN YOUR CALENDAR (color code them)
- Holidays
- Birthdays
- Vacations
- Weddings

2. Schedule when your newsletter goes out! (COLOR CODED)

3. Schedule 2 teleseminars a month! (1 will build your list and 2 will make your MONEY)
- #1 You hosting yourself as the guest speaker
- #2 You hosting a guest speaker
- Think about a name for your series – I called mine the "CATAPULT Your Business To SUPER SUCCESS in 2014 – Expert Series"

4. For each teleseminar, determine a:
- Blogging Strategy
- Email marketing campaign
- Social Media campaign
- Affiliate Marketing campaign (could be a separate calendar)
- Mobile Marketing campaign
- Combination (but be CLEAR before you start on what you are going to do so you do not get overwhelmed)

5. Put estimated product/program launch dates on the calendar (COLOR CODED)

6. For each launch determine a:
- Blogging strategy
- Email marketing campaign
- Social Media campaign
- Affiliate marketing campaign (could be a separate calendar)
- Mobile Marketing campaign
- Combination (but be CLEAR before you start on what you are going to do so you do not get overwhelmed)

7. Look at empty spots in your calendar – what will you promote at that time?
- Your lower level or basic programs
- Speaking engagements
- Affiliate marketing of other people's products

MyPersonalBusinessCoach.com

5 - Email Planning Sheet Template

- **Attention-Catching Subject:**

- **Intro with Teaser Info:**

- **What It Is:**

- **Who It Is For:**

- **What It Is About:**

- **When Product Released:**

- **Where To Buy:**

- **Why You Need It:**

- **Price:**

- **Kits:**

- **Examples:**

- **Single Product to Promote:**

- **Call to Action:**

- **P.S. Included:**

6 - GUEST INVITATION TEMPLATE

Here's a generic fill-in-the-blank email for inviting guest speakers to speak at your webinar event. Be aware, however, that the more you customize it with your own "voice" (phrasing, personality), the more successful it's likely to be.

Simply copy the box text into your own email and replace the fields:

[GUEST NAME],

I'm preparing to host a webinar on [YOUR TOPIC/WEBINAR NAME - if they're the same] for my [XXX subscribers, fellow forum members, readers, 40 million fans, etc.]. I would greatly enjoy interviewing you as my special guest during this [DURATION, WEBINAR TYPE] on [DAY, DATE, TIME, and TIME ZONE]. Would you be able to fit this into your busy schedule for [MONTH YEAR]?

I can offer you [TERMS OF COMPENSATION], and I know your readers would be fascinated by [YOUR COMPELLING REASON HIS OR HER LIST WILL LOVE THE WEBINAR].

I would also be happy to [PROMISE OF PROMOTION], as well as [RIGHTS YOU ARE GIVING THEM EXCLUSIVELY].

If this webinar sounds like one your [READERS/LIST MEMBERS/SUBSCRIBERS/ FANS] would particularly enjoy and you are able to fit it on [DAY, DATE], please let me know so I can give you access to [AFFILIATE RESOURCES, SCRIPT, MATERIAL] well in advance.

Thank you for considering my request and I hope I may look forward to working with you to bring your [READERS, SUBSCRIBERS, ETC.] this [UNIQUE SOLUTION TO THEIR PROBLEM, INSIGHT INTO THE WORLD OF..., CHANCE TO SHARE etc.] on [DAY, DATE].

Sincerely,
[YOU'RE NAME] [CONTACT INFORMATION] [TELEPHONE]

P. S. Please help yourself to a confidential "sneak peek" at the Affiliate resources I'm setting up for my guest at: [URL]

(Here you'll find a rough example of the finished product...)

Example:

Ms. Marple,

I'm preparing a webinar on "English Criminal Behavior from a Woman's Perspective" for my 20,000 active newsletter subscribers, and I would love to interview you as my guest on a one-hour, live webinar two months from now (Saturday, Sept 24 at 1:00 p.m. EST). Would that be something you could fit into your busy schedule at this time of year?

I know your readers would love to hear your responses to my research, which was hailed in "Modern Forensics" as "ground-breaking". I can offer you excellent resources for your affiliates, including PLR posts and articles, graphics, banners and templates -- here, if you'd like a quick peek -- as well as the right to repurpose and sell our interview any way you choose. (Or, if you prefer, in lieu of rights to sell/repurpose or any promotional efforts on your part, I would be happy to pay a straight $100.00 fee for your time.)

I would also love to feature you as the cover story in my weekly "Melting Pot" newsletter, two weeks before our webinar.

The webinar is set to run all weekend, in a "Summit" format, and Mary Wollstonecraft, Agatha Christie, Hildegard of Bingham and Dorothy Sayers have also agreed to guest. Time slots are currently open to negotiation, but if a particular slot is best for you, let me know as soon as you can and I'll be delighted to reserve it for you and send you a copy of the script (and questions).
I'll be in touch two weeks from now, if I don't hear from you, to follow up.

Best regards, John Watson, M. D. 221B Baker Street London, Ontario jwatson@ meltingpotnews.com (000) 000-0000

Shelley Mitchell, BA, ACC, CPM, CAPS, CAM, HCCP, COS, MORS

7 - FOLLOW UP WITH POTENTIAL GUESTS WHO HAVEN'T REPLIED TEMPLATE

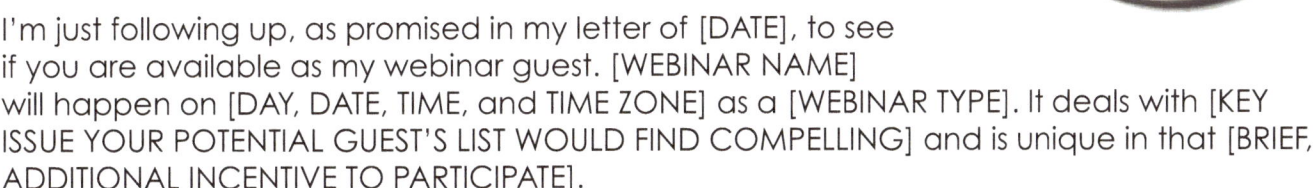

A generic and brief fill-in-the-blank email for following up with unanswered guest speaker requests reminding them to let you know if they can speak or not, etc.

[NAME],

I'm just following up, as promised in my letter of [DATE], to see if you are available as my webinar guest. [WEBINAR NAME] will happen on [DAY, DATE, TIME, and TIME ZONE] as a [WEBINAR TYPE]. It deals with [KEY ISSUE YOUR POTENTIAL GUEST'S LIST WOULD FIND COMPELLING] and is unique in that [BRIEF, ADDITIONAL INCENTIVE TO PARTICIPATE].

If I don't hear from you by [DAY, DATE], I will assume this indicates you're not available, and will approach my second choice as a guest -- no need for you to respond, unless you'd like to accept this invitation.

Thank you again for considering guesting on my webinar.

Yours sincerely, [YOUR NAME] [YOUR CONTACT INFORMATION] [PHONE OR MOBILE NUMBER]

Some suggestions for your additional incentive:

o Your subscribers themselves generated the questions o It solves the problem of [GAP YOUR WEBINAR FILLS] that [GUEST'S COMPETITORS] have not yet addressed o It gives a genuinely new twist on a universal subject o It was your own comment [QUOTE COMMENT] that inspired this [SOLUTION, PRODUCT, etc.] o It was endorsed by [CELEBRITY NAME OR AUTHORITY WEBSITE] o It was inspired by [REASON]

TIP # 1: Try not to give reasons like "My cat [ANYTHING]" -- unless you're dealing with a Cat Expert. (And probably not even then!)

Shelley Mitchell, BA, ACC, CPM, CAPS, CAM, HCCP, COS, MORS

8 - WEBINAR EMAIL ANNOUNCEMENT TEMPLATE

A generic fill-in-the-blank email announcing the webinar with link to handout and where to go, etc. Just copy the text within the table box and paste it into your own email.

(Be sure to insert your own hyperlink over the words "CLICK HERE" and "register anyway".)

- Name of Your Webinar Here
- Mark this date on your calendar: [DAY, DATE]
- Have you ever wanted to [your unique question here]? I've put together a webinar that will give you the answers you need:
- Benefit number one
  - Benefit number two
  - Benefit number three
  - Benefit number four
  - Benefit number five
- Here's what to do right now:
- [insert hyperlink-->]CLICK HERE [<--insert hyperlink] to reserve your seat.
- See you there!
- [YOUR NAME]
- PS - Even if you can't make it [day of the webinar - e.g. Tuesday], [insert hyperlink-->] register anyway [<--insert hyperlink], so you'll be able to download the recording afterwards.

9 - WEBINAR REMINDER EMAIL TEMPLATE

A generic fill-in-the-blank email reminder about your webinar. Copy the text within the box into your own email and give it your own, unique twist...

This [Day of the week -- e.g. Tuesday's] Webinar -- Its Attention-Grabbing Title as Your Headline

Time: [0:00 Time Zone -- e.g. 11:00 a.m. EST]

If you haven't already done so, now's your last chance to sign up for my [subject -- e.g. Marketing to Baby Boomers] webinar on [Day of the week -- e.g. Tuesday].

Here's what you're going to master:
• 	Repeat
• 	Your
• 	5-7
• 	Big
• 	Benefits

Even if you don't think you can make it, [insert hyperlink-->] register anyway [<--insert hyperlink]. That way, you'll get the recording to listen to at your leisure.

See you there!

[YOUR NAME]

P. S. See you [insert hyperlink-->] there [<--insert hyperlink]!

10 – SOCIAL MEDIA AND PRESS RELEASE POSTS - TEMPLATES

Fill-in-the-blank Facebook Post:
Here are two simple Facebook post formats. Simply copy the text within the box into your Facebook page and customize:

THIS [WEEK'S/MONTH'S] WEBINAR -- Day Date/Month (e.g. Tues 9/9) -- Attention-Grabbing Title of your Webinar --> http://bit.ly/link

--> Benefit in bullet point --> another great benefit your webinar offers --> Final catchy benefit

[Insert LINK to your Webinar blog post, which will display with your Facebook post, along with any graphic you inserted.]

TIP: While adding your link to your Facebook post, you can "cycle" through the graphics within your blog and select any one you choose. This is helpful if you didn't use a graphic in the post you're showcasing; or you'd like to include another blog graphic, such as your logo, instead.

Fill-in-the-blank Facebook Post:
Here are two simple Facebook post formats. Simply copy the text within the box into your Facebook page and customize:

TODAY'S WEBINAR -- "Your Catchy Webinar Title". [Time, Time Zone]. Still time to register --> http://bit.ly/link (Free recording, even if you can't "stay" today.)

N. B.: Omit the "free recording line, if (a) you're not recording it (b) you plan to actually SELL the recording.

An alternate option: "Recording FREE to participants only."

Fill-in-the-blank Blog Post:

Your blog post should be short and to the point. Create a separate tab for webinars, if you plan to make this a regular feature of your business.

Copy text within the box below. Sentences in square brackets, grayed out in lavender, are instructions only.

Omit or replace any details not relevant to your situation (i.e. don't put "Registering will also give you free access to the recording" if you're planning to sell it!)

Title of Your Webinar (in Bold): [State what your webinar is all about in one sentence.] In this [duration of webinar] webinar, you'll quickly learn:
- Why someone should do what you're proposing in the webinar
- What doing this will give/change for them
- How it will do this
- Add up to three more big benefits you want to present

[State how many "seats" there are, if it is limited-seat webinar (e.g. "There are only 25 seats for this webinar: Register below...) Omit this if it's not relevant, of course.] Register below to reserve your webinar spot:

[Your Signup Form]

Registering will also give you free access to the recording, even if you miss this particular webinar -- and you'll be notified of new, upcoming webinars.

See you there!

Shelley Mitchell, BA, ACC, CPM, CAPS, CAM, HCCP, COS, MORS

Fill-in-the-blank press release:

TIPS: Use keywords, if your press release is for an online news service. ALWAYS write press releases in the Third Person! Choose only ONE "release" option.

And, yes -- you DO include the "# # #" at the end of your press release.

FOR IMMEDIATE RELEASE / FOR RELEASE BEFORE [DATE]/ FOR RELEASE AFTER [DATE] FREE WEBINAR [Month, Date]: Title of Webinar Contact: Your name Company: Company name Address: Mailing address associated with your webinar Phone: (000) 000-0000 Email: Email address (yours or assistant who will be handling this) URL: Website that gives more information (usually media web page, if you have one)

CITY, State – Briefly summarize what the press release is about, answering the questions "Who is giving it; what it is (e.g. a virtual presentation/webinar/summit you participate in via your computer); Where it is (e.g. online); Why - what big key benefit it offers the reader -- and finally, When -- Day, month, date (e.g. Tuesday, March 15). (Keep it short and punchy; don't use adjectives or adverbs.)

Second paragraph: More information on what was said in the first paragraph, expanding one key point.

Third paragraph: Quote a former webinar participant, niche expert or even yourself (in the third person) saying why this webinar will be of particular interest to the reader or what it did for them. [Optional] Fourth paragraph: If you've already quoted someone else, add a quotation from yourself, including who you are. (E.g. "Mary Rafters, CEO of Red Bar International, states: "Learning how to barrel race is not usually something you can acquire online, but knowing the seven secrets of balance gives the racer instant power.") This paragraph should enhance and add depth to what's already been said.

Last paragraph: Factual information on where to get more information (your name, link and other relevant contact information).

# # #

Twitter Post # 1:

[Instructions: Replace all lavender text in Tweet template, below, with your own specific data.]

Have you signed up for this year's big [YOUR EVENT NAME OR SUBJECT] event yet? [#YOURHASHTAG] Find out more: [YOUR BIT.LY LINK to squeeze/signup page]

Example: Have you signed up for this year's big sports coaching event yet? Find out more #Sports2011: http://ab.cd/1eEFg

Twitter Post # 2:

[Instructions: Replace all lavender text in Tweet template, below, with your own specific data. Do not include square brackets.]

There's still time to squeeze in under the wire for this year's big [YOUR EVENT NAME OR SUBJECT] event [#YOURHASHTAG] - Grab your seat: [YOUR BIT.LY LINK to squeeze/signup page]

Example: There's still time to squeeze in under the wire for this year's big sports coaching event #Sports2011 - Grab your seat: http://ab.cd/1eEFg

Shelley Mitchell, BA, ACC, CPM, CAPS, CAM, HCCP, COS, MORS

11 - WEBINAR CHECKLIST / AGENDA

EVENT NAME/TOPIC:

TYPE: [Discussion, lesson, panel, etc.]

DATE:

PRESENTER:

GUEST(S):

RECORDING: Yes _____ No _____

15-5 minutes prior to webinar:

Final equipment check. Recording equipment READY: _____

If early birds are already waiting in the audience, let them know quickly how to mute and un-mute; then "warm" them up with informal chat. Ask:
*   Their names
*   Where they're from
*   What they're hoping to learn today/what brings them here

Also ask each one a "chatty" question: E. G. How's the weather in Colorado today? Are you enjoying the summer holidays yet?

0:00-0:00 Thanks to all audience members for taking the time to join you

Introductions - self plus guest(s)

Topic and "key question" you're going to solve [brief]

Instructions:
*   Muting
*   When questions will be answered
*   Rules, etc.
*   Whether or not recording will be available
*   Your website URL: _____

Guest's website or book URL: _____

MyPersonalBusinessCoach.com

Important incentive to stay until end of webinar:
- Exclusive Special Offer link to be given only to live webinar participants
- Free gift
- No recording available
- Only paid recording available
- Other _____

0:00-0:00 Reinforce topic and "key question" you're going to solve.

FOCUS ON AUDIENCE MEMBER wishes, needs, problems - not self or guest.

Mid-session
Briefly mention your own or guest's book/website link
Briefly refresh audience (i.e. latecomers) on your topic
Briefly re-state rules re: questions

0:00-0:00 Wrap up and final instructions (if needed)

0:00-0:00 Q & A session

0:00-0:00 "Last two questions" warning

0:00-0:00 Thank guests and audience

GIVE LINK to exclusive special offer, gift, etc.: _____

Let audience know:
- How they can give you feedback
- When to expect your next webinar _____
- Its topic _____

Sign off with your unique signature (including CALL TO ACTION: e.g. "This is Nicky Anderson, the Mominator. Join me on Saturday, August 13th at 10 a.m. Eastern Standard Time for How to Save Two Hundred Dollars on Back to School Supplies. Go mark it on your calendar right now.")

Don't forget to send your Thank you Email which includes your call to action and the recording/link.

Shelley Mitchell, BA, ACC, CPM, CAPS, CAM, HCCP, COS, MORS

12 - WEBINAR THANK YOU EMAIL TEMPLATE

A generic fill-in-the-blank email for after the webinar thanking your attendee and delivering any promised recording, downloads, links, etc.

Webinar Title and Date Here

Thanks for making time in your busy schedule to attend yesterday's Webinar on [Your Webinar Subject or Title]. I'm already getting great feedback about the material we covered!

As promised, here is [insert hyperlink-->] [your replay; your download; your handout; your special gift; other] [<--insert hyperlink]...

Really looking forward to seeing you at our next Webinar.

[insert hyperlink-->]Click Here for the Webinar Replay [<--insert hyperlink]

All the best,

[YOUR NAME]

P. S. Post your thoughts or comments about the Webinar on [blog; Facebook; Twitter, etc.]. Your valued feedback will allow me to make sure I answer all your questions.

(Or, if you prefer, you can also send questions, comments and feedback to: [email address])

Joint Teleseminar Process - When I Host Someone Else in My Teleseminar Series					
Guest:		Phone:		Email:	
Host:		Phone:		Email:	
Event Title:				Conf.#:	
Event Date:				Participant Code:	
Event Time:				Host Code:	

Items Needed	Responsible Party	Days needed Prior to Event	Date Needed	Status	Notes
Select Date, time and duration of teleseminar/webinar	Host/Guest	30			
Teleseminar title, and 3-5 bullet points describing event	Guest	30			
Consider offering a door prize at end of event	Host/Guest	20			
Create autoresponders to go to all registrants after sign up.	Host	20			
Create Facebook appropriate image to promote event	Host	20			
Create Facebook Event	Host	20			
Create Opt-In Page	Host	20			
Decide whether or not you will take live Q&A questions	Host/Guest	20			
Discuss and agree upon if and how registrant lists will be shared.	Host/Guest	20			
Discuss and agree upon terms of affiliate revenue share from guest to host.	Host/Guest	20			
Discuss and agree upon terms of discounts, bonuses, time sensitive offers and etc. to be made to registrants	Host/Guest	20			
Make a video for opt-in page	Guest	20			
Paid promotion of event on Facebook	Host/Guest	20			
Provide Guest Bio to Host	Guest	20			
Provide Guest Headshot to Host	Guest	20			
Tweet image with URL to opt-in page daily	Host/Guest	20			
Upload image to Pinterest with URL to opt-in page	Host/Guest	20			

Shelley Mitchell, BA, ACC, CPM, CAPS, CAM, HCCP, COS, MORS

Build My List, Build My Business, Build My Bank Account!

Catapult Your Business to Super Success Series Blueprint
Using List Building Strategies, Email Marketing, Webinars and much more to
Track and Watch Your Income Grow!

Items Needed	Responsible Party	Days needed Prior to Event	Date Needed	Status	Notes
Invite all friends to Facebook Event	Host/Guest	14			
Ask Facebook firends to share the event.	Host/Guest	10			
Create press release for event and release to our respective communities	Host/Guest	10			
Create series of follow-up autoresponders to registrants with audio recording, selling product, notifying of deadline for bonuses, special pricing, etc.	Host	10			
Invite all LinkedIn Connections to event.	Host/Guest	10			
Promote blog post throughout all social media outlets.	Host/Guest	10			
Send invitation to your list with opt-in URL.	Host/Guest	10			
Write blog post about teleseminar topic. Last paragraph invites them to join event with URL to opt-in page. Include image in post.	Host/Guest	10			
Determine call to action at end of teleseminar.	Host/Guest	8			
Provide script of interview questions and outline of answers to host.	Guest	8			
Provide teleseminar delivery platform (Instant Teleseminar, GoToMeeting, etc.)	Host	8			
Provide teleseminar/webinar dial in and password to guest.	Host	8			
If call to action will be a product, provide affiliate sales page URL to host	Guest	5			
Provide teleseminar handout or slides to host.	Guest	3			
After teleseminar, tell host who purchased so they can be removed from autoresponder series.	Guest	0			

MyPersonalBusinessCoach.com

Shelley Mitchell, BA, ACC, CPM, CAPS, CAM, HCCP, COS, MORS

ABOUT THE AUTHOR - Shelley Mitchell

FUN, FEARLESS, FOCUSED... Shelley is an expert in Entrepreneurial Coaching and her mission is in helping Smart, Driven, Creative Entrepreneurs get Un-Stuck, Un-Stressed and Out of Overwhelm so they can create their VISION, develop their PLAN, FOCUS on their PRIORITIES, and take ACTION to build their businesses, make more money and reach their dreams and goals.

President/CEO of My Personal Business Coach LLC and My Personal ADHD Coach, Creator of the Right Brain Solution (productivity tools for creative entrepreneurs) and Author of the forthcoming Book Series "How to Get & Keep What you Really, Really Want". As a woman of many talents with a stellar success record of over 23 years starting and running small to multi-million dollar businesses, she understands how passion, drive, and commitment have made it possible to live her best life and how it has put her in a unique position, which allows her to serve her clients in extraordinary ways. Her formal education and certifications along with her vast experience make her one of the most unique and top business consultants/coaches in the country.

EXPERIENCE - She is a Certified Business Coach and Certified ADHD/ADD Coach, having trained with Franklin Covey, Jack Canfield, Coach Training Institute, ADDCA, Direct Selling Women's Association and several others. Other formal education includes her first degree in Marketing and then going on to attain a BA in Business Management and Finance and MBA work in Finance and Human Resources. Her vast life and business experiences, coupled with her desire to continuously grow and improve have positioned her at the top of her field and allow her to serve her clients in the most extraordinary way. Her experience includes 23 years' experience in real estate development and management with numerous industry related designations and passionate involvement in educating others. She was a Vice-President with several management companies and also has a unique contrast with a gleaming successful record in direct sales with several companies earning awards as Top Recruiter and Top Sales and reaching Leadership levels in record times. Shelley as served in the US Army as a Sergeant, holding two combat patches for operations in Panama and Saudi Arabia. In 1992, Cosmopolitan Magazine and Helen Gurley Brown named her their mascot and *The Fun Fearless Female Column* was created with Shelley being the first.

ADHD & HER SON - During her successful dual career in Real Estate and Direct Sales, she

MyPersonalBusinessCoach.com

learned how to make things happen even when ADHD/ADD got in the way. Being strong and overcoming obstacles were always here strength but she soon learned the same effect could be achieved by organizing one's efforts around a central purpose, identifying goals and objectives to drive a person's daily activities. She was inspired to become a coach to help others including her son who struggled with overcoming the same issues with ADHD but due to a medical condition, couldn't be conventionally treated. At just 16 years old, he overcame a tremendous amount of challenges, started his own business www.CalebsWord.com and became a speaker and published Author of his own book "7 Days to Understanding Your Teen" and they are now both part of this very special Mother/Son entrepreneurial team on a mission to serve and elevate others in overcoming challenges and reaching their dreams and goals.

SPEAKING & TEACHING - As an Inspirational Speaker and energetic Trainer, Shelley has spoken before national organizations and taught classes on specific industry related material including Thinking Outside the Box, Goal Setting, DISC, Successful Closing Techniques, and How to Pass a Shop and currently speaks regularly on hot topics such as Time Management & Productivity, Marketing& Branding, Leadership, Increasing Sales Revenues, Networking, Customer Service, Business Planning, Budgeting, Entrepreneurship and How to Start and Grow Your Own Business. She also specializes in *"Finding the Magic Wand That Gets Your New Recruits to Pull Rabbits out of Their Own Hats"* which is one of her signature talks for Direct Sales leaders who want to build their teams. She also serves as an Adjunct Professor at Palm Beach State College for the Center of Leadership and develops custom programs for businesses and corporations.

INVOLVEMENT - Shelley has also always been very involved in her community with past experiences serving on the City Council, Rotary Club, BNI and the Chamber. Today, she is a very active member and Committee Chair in the Junior League of Boca Raton and a Chapter Leader for the Women's Prosperity Network in Palm Beach/Boca Raton. At Shelley's first event with WPN Global, she knew she had come home to a community of women who were just as 'not normal' as she was, that is: women defining success on their own terms and supporting each other in business and in life where each and every person in WPN was genuinely interested in EACH OTHER's success. She also serves on the WORKPLACE Committee nationally for ADDA (Attention Deficit Disorder Association)

PASSIONS - Her passions include her family, travel, sky diving, scuba diving, Golf, boating, and truly helping others get clear on their plan, focus on their priorities and take action to grow their business and reach their dreams and goals.

Shelley Mitchell, BA, ACC, CPM, CAPS, CAM, HCCP, COS, MORS

Build My List, Build My Business, Build My Bank Account!

Catapult Your Business to Super Success Series Blueprint
Using List Building Strategies, Email Marketing, Webinars and much more to
Track and Watch Your Income Grow!

Please be sure to visit Shelley's website: **MyPersonalBusinessCoach.com** and connect with her on
Facebook **CLICK HERE**

If you would like to discover if she might be a great coach for you, please email Shelley Mitchell to arrange a time to talk and take advantage of a complimentary 20 minute Strategy Session.

Have a Fun, Fearless & FOCUSED Day!

Shelley Mitchell, BA, ACC, CPM, CAPS, CAM, HCCP, COS, MORS

APPOINTMENT LINK HERE: To set up an Appointment, please **CLICK HERE**
or visit: http://www.vcita.com/v/mypersonalbusinesscoach/online_scheduling#/services

(Author of the forthcoming book series "How to Get (and keep) what You Really, Really Want" and Creator of the RIGHT BRAIN SOLUTION - tools for the creative entrepreneur)

President - *My Personal Business Coach & My Personal ADHD Coach*
Office: 561-320-1517 email: shelley@mypersonalbusinesscoach.com
Website: http://www.mypersonalbusinesscoach.com/
Like us on FACEBOOK: https://www.facebook.com/MyPersonalBusinessCoach
skype: mitchell.shelley Twitter: @MyPrsnlBizCoach

CLICK THE PHOTO BELOW TO GET YOUR FREE WEEKLY SUCCESS PLANNER

or visit
https://av155.infusionsoft.com/app/form/21c0c04969dd3131b0ba2f230f40fda8

MyPersonalBusinessCoach.com

Joint Teleseminar Process - When I Host Someone Else in My Teleseminar Series					
Guest:		Phone:		Email:	
Host:		Phone:		Email:	
Event Title:				Conf.#:	
Event Date:				Participant Code:	
Event Time:				Host Code:	

Items Needed	Responsible Party	Days needed Prior to Event	Date Needed	Status	Notes
Select Date, time and duration of teleseminar/webinar	Host/Guest	30			
Teleseminar title, and 3-5 bullet points describing event	Guest	30			
Consider offering a door prize at end of event	Host/Guest	20			
Create autoresponders to go to all registrants after sign up.	Host	20			
Create Facebook appropriate image to promote event	Host	20			
Create Facebook Event	Host	20			
Create Opt-In Page	Host	20			
Decide whether or not you will take live Q&A questions	Host/Guest	20			
Discuss and agree upon if and how registrant lists will be shared.	Host/Guest	20			
Discuss and agree upon terms of affiliate revenue share from guest to host.	Host/Guest	20			
Discuss and agree upon terms of discounts, bonuses, time sensitive offers and etc. to be made to registrants	Host/Guest	20			
Make a video for opt-in page	Guest	20			
Paid promotion of event on Facebook	Host/Guest	20			
Provide Guest Bio to Host	Guest	20			
Provide Guest Headshot to Host	Guest	20			
Tweet image with URL to opt-in page daily	Host/Guest	20			
Upload image to Pinterest with URL to opt-in page	Host/Guest	20			

Shelley Mitchell, BA, ACC, CPM, CAPS, CAM, HCCP, COS, MORS

Build My List, Build My Business, Build My Bank Account!
Catapult Your Business to Super Success Series Blueprint
Using List Building Strategies, Email Marketing, Webinars and much more to
Track and Watch Your Income Grow!

Items Needed	Responsible Party	Days needed Prior to Event	Date Needed	Status	Notes
Invite all friends to Facebook Event	Host/Guest	14			
Ask Facebook firends to share the event.	Host/Guest	10			
Create press release for event and release to our respective communities	Host/Guest	10			
Create series of follow-up autoresponders to registrants with audio recording, selling product, notifying of deadline for bonuses, special pricing, etc.	Host	10			
Invite all LinkedIn Connections to event.	Host/Guest	10			
Promote blog post throughout all social media outlets.	Host/Guest	10			
Send invitation to your list with opt-in URL.	Host/Guest	10			
Write blog post about teleseminar topic. Last paragraph invites them to join event with URL to opt-in page. Include image in post.	Host/Guest	10			
Determine call to action at end of teleseminar.	Host/Guest	8			
Provide script of interview questions and outline of answers to host.	Guest	8			
Provide teleseminar delivery platform (Instant Teleseminar, GoToMeeting, etc.)	Host	8			
Provide teleseminar/webinar dial in and password to guest.	Host	8			
If call to action will be a product, provide affiliate sales page URL to host	Guest	5			
Provide teleseminar handout or slides to host.	Guest	3			
After teleseminar, tell host who purchased so they can be removed from autoresponder series.	Guest	0			

MyPersonalBusinessCoach.com

Joint Teleseminar Process - When I Host Someone Else in My Teleseminar Series

Guest:	Phone:	Email:
Host:	Phone:	Email:
Event Title:		Conf.#:
Event Date:		Participant Code:
Event Time:		Host Code:

Items Needed	Responsible Party	Days needed Prior to Event	Date Needed	Status	Notes
Select Date, time and duration of teleseminar/webinar	Host/Guest	30			
Teleseminar title, and 3-5 bullet points describing event	Guest	30			
Consider offering a door prize at end of event	Host/Guest	20			
Create autoresponders to go to all registrants after sign up.	Host	20			
Create Facebook appropriate image to promote event	Host	20			
Create Facebook Event	Host	20			
Create Opt-In Page	Host	20			
Decide whether or not you will take live Q&A questions	Host/Guest	20			
Discuss and agree upon if and how registrant lists will be shared.	Host/Guest	20			
Discuss and agree upon terms of affiliate revenue share from guest to host.	Host/Guest	20			
Discuss and agree upon terms of discounts, bonuses, time sensitive offers and etc. to be made to registrants	Host/Guest	20			
Make a video for opt-in page	Guest	20			
Paid promotion of event on Facebook	Host/Guest	20			
Provide Guest Bio to Host	Guest	20			
Provide Guest Headshot to Host	Guest	20			
Tweet image with URL to opt-in page daily	Host/Guest	20			
Upload image to Pinterest with URL to opt-in page	Host/Guest	20			

Shelley Mitchell, BA, ACC, CPM, CAPS, CAM, HCCP, COS, MORS

Build My List, Build My Business, Build My Bank Account!
Catapult Your Business to Super Success Series Blueprint
Using List Building Strategies, Email Marketing, Webinars and much more to
Track and Watch Your Income Grow!

Items Needed	Responsible Party	Days needed Prior to Event	Date Needed	Status	Notes
Invite all friends to Facebook Event	Host/Guest	14			
Ask Facebook firends to share the event.	Host/Guest	10			
Create press release for event and release to our respective communities	Host/Guest	10			
Create series of follow-up autoresponders to registrants with audio recording, selling product, notifying of deadline for bonuses, special pricing, etc.	Host	10			
Invite all LinkedIn Connections to event.	Host/Guest	10			
Promote blog post throughout all social media outlets.	Host/Guest	10			
Send invitation to your list with opt-in URL.	Host/Guest	10			
Write blog post about teleseminar topic. Last paragraph invites them to join event with URL to opt-in page. Include image in post.	Host/Guest	10			
Determine call to action at end of teleseminar.	Host/Guest	8			
Provide script of interview questions and outline of answers to host.	Guest	8			
Provide teleseminar delivery platform (Instant Teleseminar, GoToMeeting, etc.)	Host	8			
Provide teleseminar/webinar dial in and password to guest.	Host	8			
If call to action will be a product, provide affiliate sales page URL to host	Guest	5			
Provide teleseminar handout or slides to host.	Guest	3			
After teleseminar, tell host who purchased so they can be removed from autoresponder series.	Guest	0			

MyPersonalBusinessCoach.com

www.ingramcontent.com/pod-product-compliance
Lightning Source LLC
Chambersburg PA
CBHW040745200526
45159CB00023B/1739